THE SECRET WAR ON AMERICA'S CREDIT UNIONS

BY
MICHAEL MCKELLY

ISBN: 1494797984
ISBN-13: 9781494797980

DEDICATION

This pamphlet is for the hard-working activists
in the American credit union movement.

Table of Contents

ACKNOWLEDGMENTS

I wish to thank the National Credit Union Association and the
Texas Credit Union League for their assistance and
support in the creation of this advocacy pamphlet.

A Secret War

A long-simmering feud between the nation's bankers and credit unions rose to rapid boil in 1998, when the U.S Supreme Court found in favor of banks and their trade association in a suit that sought to limit the ability of credit unions to expand their fields of membership.[1] In their ruling, the court held that credit unions must focus on a single common bond amongst their membership. Six months later, however, President Clinton signed a law which reversed the court's ruling, allowing credit unions to have multiple unrelated fields of membership.[2] This reversal, no doubt, only stoked flames fueling the feud between the bankers and credit unions.

The following year, in 1999, the American Bankers Association (ABA) sued the National Credit Union Administration (NCUA), claiming that their member credit unions were violating the intent of the new 1998 law. That suit was dismissed by the U.S. Appeals Court in 2001, further frustrating the agenda of the ABA.

The bankers continued to wage their war on credit unions on three major tactical fronts. Their talking points consistently raised the following three issues:[3]

1. The bankers claim that it is unfair for credit unions to be exempt from federal income taxes, while banks are subject to taxes which can be as high as 35% of their earnings.

2. They say that credit unions have expanded beyond their original purpose, beyond the mission of making loans to those who have historically had difficulty getting loans from banks.

3. They assert if credit unions want to offer the same kinds of services as banks, they should be regulated in exactly the same way, by the same agencies. This particular argument usually centers on the Community Reinvestment Act (CRA), which requires bankers to make loans to low-income groups and distressed neighborhoods.[4]

For the sake of simplicity, these three issues can easily be rolled into one over-arching battle cry: *unfair competition.* With the collapse of some of the nation's largest and most powerful banks in the financial crisis of 2007-2010, their battle cry has become even more shrill. As the most affected banks begin their recovery from a debacle that left the nation's credit unions relatively untouched, (and in many cases, stronger) bankers are renewing their calls for federal taxation of credit unions, and increased limits on their ability of credit unions to compete in the financial services marketplace.[5]

During this onslaught of attacks by the ABA and its member-bankers, most in the credit union movement have practiced "armadillo tactics," trying to make themselves smaller targets and attempting to appear non-threatening to their banking brethren. Even though credit union organizations across the country scrambled to ratchet up their lobbying efforts in congress, their local public relations responses were generally non-existent, or muted at best. Credit union officials, eager to maintain good relations with business leaders in communities dominated by bankers, would often decline to respond publicly in any way to the bankers' attacks.

Unfortunately, this "armadillo response" has led to a situation where many of the allegations by the ABA have circulated in the media virtually unchallenged. This is doubly unfortunate, considering the fact that so many of the arguments they deploy are distortions at best and, in many instances, outright fabrications.

Do Credit Unions Pay Taxes?

Consider even the most the basic allegation, that "credit unions don't pay taxes." The public has heard this claim so often that it has gained a certain patina of credibility. The plain truth is, credit unions *do* pay taxes. Credit unions, depending on whether they are federally or state chartered credit unions and the state where they are located, pay federal payroll taxes, unrelated business income tax (UBIT), state corporate income taxes, state payroll taxes, state and local sales taxes, local real property taxes, local personal property taxes, excise taxes, franchise taxes, use taxes, licenses and permit fees.

Credit unions, whether federally or state chartered, are exempt only from the federal corporate income tax. This exemption was established by congress in 1937, affirmed by statute in 1951, and re-affirmed in 1998 in H.R. 1151, the Credit Union Membership Access Act. [6]

It is important to note that credit unions are member-owned cooperatives that *return a greater percentage of their revenues than banks do* to their depositors in the form of *dividends*. This income for the members of credit unions is documented and reported annually. Credit unions issue each member an IRS Form 1099, and those members are responsible for paying the personal income taxes on that income, in much the same way that stockholders in for-profit S-corporations pay income taxes on the income they derive as stockholders.

Why is this important? *Read on.*

Pot, Meet Kettle

Fact: 2,438 U.S. Banks Pay No Corporate Income Taxes At All

It is perhaps ironic that, while bankers are heavily invested in vilifying credit unions for having an exemption to the federal income tax, they simultaneously and diligently work to identify legal loopholes, tax havens, and restructuring schemes to significantly reduce the federal income taxes that *they* pay.

For example, on January 1, 1997, thanks to the Small Business Job Protection Act of 1996, which was signed into law by President Bill Clinton, commercial banks became eligible to elect to be taxed under Subchapter S of Chapter A of the Internal Revenue Code of 1986 (commonly referred to as an S-Corporation). This election allows a corporation to be considered a partnership for federal income tax purposes. The immediate impact of the new law was to allow some banks to elect to become S-corporations and pay no federal income tax.

In 1997, the first year, 561 banks converted to S corporations in order to become tax exempt.[7]

By 2003, eight banks and seven thrifts with assets totaling *over $1 billion each* had become S-corporations, [8] and by the first quarter of 2005, no less than 20 percent of *all* banks with less than $100 million in assets had elected to become S-corporations.[9]

Today, there are 2,438 S-corporation banks in the U.S., or *roughly one third of all banks.* [10] Not all of these S-corporation banks are small ones. The largest, according to the FDIC, has over $12 billion in assets, which is notable, considering the benefits of S-corporations were designed to help America's *small businesses.*

This stampede on the part of so many community banks to gain tax-exempt status highlights the hypocrisy of their many arguments outlining the evils of such an exemption. But more importantly, many banks did *not* opt for the tax exemption, mainly because *it was more profitable to forego the exemption in favor of a more lucrative regulatory environment.*

There are "strings attached" to the tax exemption that comes from electing to become an S-corporation, limitations that are very similar to the environment under which credit unions must operate. An S-corporation bank must be headquartered in the United States and cannot have more than hundred stockholders. Each stockholder must be an individual, an estate, a qualified plan, or a specific type of tax-exempt organization. Nonresident aliens cannot be stockholders in S-corporation banks. S-corporation banks can have only one class of stock and cannot use the reserve method for accounting for loan losses.

The limitations on S-corporation banks impose unique constraints on a bank's operating strategy. For example, because they are limited to one hundred stockholders, they have reduced access to new capital by simply attracting more stockholders. To fund any significant growth, the S-corporation bank *must earn it and retain it* (like a credit union), or raise capital via new equity offerings to a limited number of existing stockholders. [11]

The slower and more difficult growth that comes with electing to become a tax-exempt S-corporation bank is the *major* factor in why the larger banks (which are less likely to become S-corporations) have taken market share away from the smaller community banks while pointing the finger at credit unions as the culprit! [12]

The ABA has been unable to clearly articulate why the nation's S-corporation community banks have continued to lose market share to their bigger brethren banks, despite enjoying the same kind of tax advantage that applies to credit unions.

The So-called "Unfair Advantage"

Myth: The Income Tax Exemption Gives Credit Unions an *Unfair Advantage*

If credit unions have such an "unfair" advantage over banks, why is it that we have not seen more banks convert to credit union charters? There are few, if any barriers to doing so. The easy answer, of course, is that no banker wants to accept the significantly lower salaries that credit unions pay their management, few banks would embrace the democratic ownership and volunteer control that credit unions enjoy, and finally, the regulatory environment that credit unions must operate in is *much* more restrictive *and less profitable* than the one that most bankers enjoy.

A 2003 study by the Kansas City Federal Reserve bank observed 1,050 community banks, made up of 777 C-Corp banks, and 273 S-Corp banks, distributed across low, medium, and high-growth counties in seven states in the Midwest and the Rocky Mountains region. Their study found that the growth and performance of the S-Corp banks was similar to that of the C-Corp banks,[13] suggesting that *a federal income tax exemption offers no significant advantage, given the inherent limitations that come with such an exemption.*

Nevertheless, the bankers continue to repeat the mantra that the federal income tax exemption for credit unions gives the credit unions an *unfair advantage.* Let's take a look at the effects of this so-called advantage on credit unions and their share of deposits.

16

Credit unions now account for only 6.2% of the combined assets of all depository institutions in the United States. Assuming the current growth rates of the past decade going forward, it will take until the year *2053* for the credit union share of total deposits to climb to just 10% of the market.[14] Other types of businesses in other markets would no doubt love to have "competition" that is so benign!

According to the Federal Deposit Insurance Corporation (FDIC) and the National Credit Union Administration (NCUA), the market share of assets held by community and smaller regional banks (defined as all but the top 100 banks in the US) has indeed *fallen by almost 50%* from 1992 to 2004. Note that the credit union market share of deposits has remained level at about 6% throughout that same period.

The inconvenient truth is, during this same period, as community banks lost half of their market share and the credit unions' share remained level, the largest 100 banks in the nation increased their share by 63%. Their share of deposits grew from 41% in 1992 to 67% in 2004.[15]

If *anyone* is competing unfairly with America's smaller community banks, it is that group comprised *of the largest 100 banks in the nation, and not the credit union movement!*

Credit Unions vs. Savings & Loans

Myth: Credit Unions Should Be Taxed Just Like Savings & Loans (S&Ls)

Truth: There *are* major differences between credit unions and Savings & Loans (S&Ls). For example, it is possible for an S&L to be a joint stock company, or even publicly traded. Another difference is that by law, thrifts must have at least 65 percent of their lending in mortgages and other consumer loans

The argument that credit unions should be subject to the same regulatory model as Savings and Loans, or mutual savings banks, inexplicably continues to gain traction in legislative circles, despite what we've learned from the past.

60 years ago, American bankers attempted to eliminate a potential threat to their corporate profits – the Savings and Loans, by successfully lobbying Congress to strip them of their tax-exempt status.   Congress did so, saying, "At the present time, mutual savings banks are in active competition with commercial banks and life insurance companies for the public savings, and they compete with many types of taxable institutions in the security and real estate markets... the continuance of the tax-free treatment now accorded mutual savings banks would be discriminatory."[16]

The results were disastrous. While it is undeniable that there were many *other* factors that contributed to the next four decades of turmoil in the savings and loan industry, including a challenging interest rate environment, overregulation, and later, under-regulation, the fact remains that by 1981, 85% of all savings and loans were *losing money*. In a misguided effort to "save" the S&Ls in the early eighties, congress passed regulations that had exactly the *opposite* effect, encouraging the risky and corrupt behaviors that resulted in the S&L crisis of the late 1980s.[17]

According to the Cato Institute, there were 4,500 S&Ls in America in 1979. Just thirteen years later, in 1992, only 1,800 S&Ls remained, amounting to an astounding 60% loss.[18] This precipitous drop is *not* simply the result of consolidations and mergers. From 1975 to 1990, the savings & loans' market share of single-family mortgage loans plummeted from 53% to 30%.[19]

Is *this* the vision that the ABA has for America's credit unions?

Unprecedented Growth?

Myth: The CU Tax Exemption is What Enables Their "Unprecedented Growth"

The so-called "unprecedented growth" of credit unions is highly debatable on its face, and it is also a very carefully worded claim that avoids any mention of *how it compares to the growth of banks.*

To illustrate how this *verbal slight-of-hand* is accomplished, consider the fact that credit unions have seen a significant decline in the number of adult members in their prime borrowing years. The number of members between the ages of 25 and 44 years old has declined from 55% of all members to 38% of members between 1985 and 2006. Overall credit union memberships should increase by nearly 5 million 2010, but it is estimated that the number of members in the prime borrowing age demographic (25-44 years old) will decline by *2.5 million* in the same year.[20]

In 1991, credit union membership growth was just 1.1% - which failed to even keep pace with the growth of the U.S. population. From 2000 to 2005, the nationwide average annual membership growth rate for credit unions was effectively flat - a mere 1.7%.

In 2006, the average small credit union (less than $5M in assets) had a 1.6% *decline* in membership, while the average large credit union (more than $100M in assets) had a pitiful 3.4% increase in membership.

According to the NCUA, the nation's credit unions have dropped in number from over 10,000 in the year 2001 to just 7600 by the second quarter of 2010 – a 24% decrease in the number of credit unions in just nine years.

Deposits and assets of credit unions *have* shown slow growth in recent years, however, they pale in comparison when viewed side-by-side with matching statistics for *banks*. No one could claim, with any credibility, that the low-growth of deposits and assets and the no-growth in membership and overall number of credit unions could be called a "good" thing. Therefore, the bankers resort to calling it "unprecedented growth," hoping that the general public and their elected officials will assume (incorrectly) that it must be unprecedented *positive growth!*.

Some bankers have apparently begun to believe their own propaganda, claiming in various forums that "credit unions are growing by leaps and bounds."[21] If we assume that this claim refers to the supposed threat that the slow-growth of credit union deposits and assets poses to banks, then perhaps we should take a look at those numbers.

The three largest credit unions in the country, in terms of assets, are Navy Federal CU with $41.5 billion, State Employees FCU with $21 billion and Pentagon FCU with $14.3 billion.[22] The combined assets of these three largest credit unions total $103 billion. Compare that to the single largest bank in the nation, Bank of America, with assets of $2.3 *trillion dollars,* or in simpler terms, one bank with roughly *227 times the assets of the three largest credit unions combined!*

In fact, Bank of America's assets, alone, are roughly *3 times* the total assets of *all of America's credit unions combined* ($896 billion)! This is somewhat akin to McDonald's Corporation claiming "unfair competition" from the corner hot dog stand!

The only thing "unfair" about these comparisons is the fact that they are made at *all,* with little or no verification of their veracity. Let's examine some of the other allegations that have been tossed around, hoping that no one will check the facts.

A Taxpayer's Burden?

Myth: The CU Tax Exemption Costs Taxpayers $31 Billion Annually

Bankers claim that "as credit union membership expands, so does the cost to American taxpayers, who underwrite the credit union industry's tax subsidy." [23]   They carefully avoid mentioning that any additional tax on America's credit unions will be an additional tax on the American consumer, since credit unions would be forced to pass along the cost to their members. The end result would be higher fees and loan rates, as well as lower dividends paid out to members everywhere.

This argument by the bankers is perhaps the most insidious of them all, pretending to show concern for the purported "costs" of the current tax exemption to taxpayers, *while actually raising costs for those who can afford it least.*

It has often been said that "corporations don't pay taxes, their customers do." But what, *exactly,* does that mean? Remember, most corporations exist to make a profit. When taxes on corporations rise, they try to reduce their costs and/or raise consumer prices to ensure that profit levels remain where they are. Since business expenses tend to remain constant and generally outside of their control, the end result is *almost always higher prices for consumers.*

According to the Tax Foundation, a research and lobbying group that is often cited by the ABA, the average American household shoulders a *corporate tax burden* of $3,190 annually, even though they technically *aren't subject* to corporate income taxes. For the poorest 20 percent of households, their share of the corporate income tax burden is actually higher than the average amount they actually pay in *individual* income taxes. Households earning under $23,700 in 2004 paid $271 in passed-on corporate income taxes (in the form of higher costs for goods and services), compared to just $171 in individual income taxes. [24]

To frame this example in even simpler terms, consider McDonalds Corporation, whose annual net profit margin in 2009 was 20.1%.[25] Imagine for a moment that McDonalds is a tax-exempt company, earning the same net profits of 20 cents on every dollar it brings in. Suddenly, a 35% income tax is imposed on the company. The company has two choices. They can either pay the tax off the bottom line, and operate at a 15% loss for the year, or they can raise their prices by 35% in order to maintain their net profit margin, and satisfy their stockholders, who have invested in the company for the sole purpose of earning a return on their investment.

Since, in reality, McDonalds *is* operating at a net profit, it can logically be deduced that they have chosen the latter option, which means that approximately thirty-five cents of the cost of every dollar-menu double cheeseburger sold at McDonalds goes towards McDonalds' corporate income tax bill.

The ABA has often leveled the charge that the credit union exemption amounts to a subsidy by the federal government which has "cost" the American taxpayer $31 billion over the past ten years. This argument is invalid on its face, because it *proceeds from the premise* that credit unions *should* be taxed, therefore, any taxes that are not collected are, somehow, *"lost."* This is a little like saying that the federal government "subsidizes" all churches and religions, and that it is somehow *losing money* because churches are not subject to income taxes.

Another example of this sort of false reasoning (based on an invalid premise) would be to claim that *if* the government should be taxing our breathing, then they are *"losing"* an huge amount of money, based on the number of breaths we take each year. The argument is absurd on its face, however, because the bankers omit the all-important *"if,"* the invalid premise often goes unchallenged.

Unfortunately, there seems to be no limit to the absurdity of the many variations on the theme that credit unions are receiving an "unfair government subsidy." This is particularly true in light of the recent Federal Troubled Assets Relief Program (TARP) for banks, which came with an *actual price tag* of at *least* $245 billion to American taxpayers, *not* in tax breaks, but in *cold, hard cash.*

The Office of Management and Budget estimates that taxpayers will lose $105 billion on its TARP "investments," and as of September 2010, the list of "deadbeat banks" has grown to over 115 banks skipping their TARP dividend payments on $3.6 billion worth of borrowings from the U.S. Treasury Department. [26] Again, the hypocrisy of the ABA's arguments against credit union "subsidies," in light of the massive government cash bailouts of banks, seems to know no bounds.

The most recent variation on this theme has taken the form of carefully orchestrated headlines decrying the September 2010 federal "bailout" of credit unions.[27] In publications like The Wall Street Journal and other forums which traditionally show a favorable bias to bankers, very little space is dedicated to explaining that the so-called "bailout" consists primarily of a National Credit Union Administration (NCUA) plan to issue $30 billion to $35 billion in government-guaranteed bonds. In other words, unlike the TARP bailout for banks, this program will *not* be primarily funded by taxpayers.

The public relations smear-campaign also avoids mentioning, whenever possible, that the so-called credit union bailout is for the *wholesale* credit union system, sometimes referred to as the "corporate credit unions." These corporate credit unions, of which there are about 27 in the nation, do *not* serve the general public. Corporate credit unions evolved to do for retail credit unions what they cannot do for themselves, whether it is due to restrictive regulations or high costs relative to their asset-size. In other words, the corporate (or wholesale) credit unions more closely resemble banks than they do a typical retail credit union. This similarity in structure and function is largely responsible for why they are now suffering from many of the same problems as banks. If anything, it *may* be considered strong argument for the premise that forcing credit unions to act like banks will *cause* more problems than it *solves*.

To counter some of the negative and often erroneous publicity that has been distributed, the NCUA has developed a series of presentations designed to help the public to better understand corporate credit unions and NCUA's latest strategy for dealing with the corporate credit union crisis, which was announced by the NCUA Board on September 24, 2010.

Chairman Debbie Matz explained, "I recognize that the complexities of this crisis have been difficult to grasp – even for those who are very familiar with the internal workings of the credit union system. NCUA has designed this series [of presentations] to provide... a broad overview, in simple terms, of all aspects of corporate credit unions – including the resolution of impaired securities... that have been a significant drain on the credit union system." [28]

The presentations, which are available for download at the NCUA website, are divided into four tracks, or issues:

- Track 1: The history of corporate credit unions and the services they have provided to consumer credit unions for the past 40 years.

- Track 2: The events that led several corporate credit unions to discover severely distressed assets on their balance sheets, and the resulting impact on consumer credit unions.

- Track 3: The actions that NCUA implemented to help stabilize the corporate credit unions.

- Track 4: The corporate resolution strategy implemented by the NCUA Board to deal with legacy assets.

The NCUA recommends that consumer credit union management teams and board members watch the presentations together and discuss them to ensure an adequate understanding of the complex issues involved and the public relations pitfalls that may be encountered. [29]

Local Tax Revenues

Myth: The CU Tax Exemption Deprives Local Governments of Needed Revenue

This red-herring of an issue has been raised by the bankers in various publications that claim that *"local municipalities... will be bearing a disproportionate burden until the... credit unions are taxed and regulated the same as... community banks."* [30] This clumsy argument doesn't even *attempt* to explain *how* a *federal tax exemption* results in lost revenue for local governments.

Again, this bears repeating : Most credit unions pay federal payroll taxes, unrelated business income tax (UBIT), state corporate income taxes, state payroll taxes, state and local sales taxes, local real property taxes, local personal property taxes, excise taxes, franchise taxes, use taxes, licenses and permit fees.

It is perhaps *conceivable* that a *weak* argument could be made that *some* states base their state income tax assessments on a corporation's federal income tax returns. However, if such is the case, and that practice results in tax savings for some corporations (to include credit unions and S-corporation banks), then it is a result of the shortsightedness of those states' legislators and tax officials.

One can hardly blame any taxpayer, whether an individual or corporation, for calculating their taxes according to the law and legally minimizing their tax liabilities whenever possible. That isn't illegal or unethical, it's *smart*.

"Not Acting Like Credit Unions"

Myth: Some Larger Credit Unions Are "No Longer Acting Like Credit Unions"

The bankers often say that they aren't after the smaller community credit unions. They just want the *largest* credit unions, the ones who have "stopped acting like credit unions" to pay *their* fair share of taxes. This argument simply doesn't hold water, however, when you look at the facts.

The largest credit unions in the country are still tiny compared to the largest banks. The three largest credit unions, Navy Federal Credit Union, State Employee Federal Credit Union, and Pentagon Federal Credit Union each has a very clearly defined field of membership (FOM) with very uniquely defined common bonds. One would also be hard-pressed to claim that those military members or state employees are a privileged elite class of depositor with unusually high incomes. Perhaps the bankers' *real* definition of *"not acting like a credit union"* is actually code for *"prospering."*

Even if one accepts the bogus argument that the bankers are *only* gunning for *"the biggest and baddest"* of the nation's credit unions, it is inevitable that any revocation of the credit union tax exemption would undoubtedly affect *all* credit unions, large *and* small.

The compliance costs involved and tax liabilities would necessarily to be passed-on to the credit unions' depositors, including those who *can least afford it.* Two of the three largest credit unions in the nation serve military members and their families, many of whom subsist at, or near, the poverty level while their loved ones are deployed to fight our wars overseas.

The bankers have employed an age-old tactic of redefining the meanings of words, phrases, and institutions to suit their own purposes. They utilize Orwellian "doublethink" to disseminate misinformation as well as anti- credit union propaganda in an effort to influence legislation and redefine the issues to their advantage. George Orwell said it best in his essay, *Politics and the English Language:* "If thought corrupts language, language can also corrupt thought."

In their unceasing efforts to influence the thoughts (and votes) of legislators, American bankers have narrowly defined *"not acting like credit unions"* as:

- Offering a full suite of financial services
- Making more small business loans and a wider variety of mortgages
- Widening their fields of membership (FOM)
- Prospering and/or growing in membership or asset-size

Perhaps it would be more useful to define how credit unions *are* supposed to act, as defined [31] by Title 12 of the U.S. Code (Banks and Banking):

- Credit unions differ from banks and other financial institutions in that the members who have accounts in the credit union are the owners of the credit union"
- [32]Only a member of a credit union may deposit money with the credit union, or borrow money from it. [33]

- Credit Unions elect their board of directors in a democratic one-person-one-vote system regardless of the amount of money invested in the credit union. [34]

- A credit union's policies governing interest rates and other matters are set by a volunteer Board of Directors elected by and from the membership itself. [35]

- Credit unions offer many of the same financial services as banks, sometimes using different terminology.

- Credit unions traditionally market themselves as providing superior member service and being committed to helping members improve their financial health.

When one applies *these* standards to the nation's credit unions, whether they be large or small, it becomes clear that they are, indeed, *acting like credit unions*, both in the spirit as well as the letter of the law.

President Abraham Lincoln once asked, "How many legs does a dog have, if you call the tail a leg? Answer: *Four.* Calling a tail a leg doesn't *make* it a leg." The lesson to be learned here is, one should never let the *bankers* define what it is to be a *credit union*.

"Not Playing By the Same Rules"

Myth: Credit Unions Don't "Play by the Same Rules" as Banks

The exact wording of this charge is always carefully crafted, and usually goes something like: "Federal- and state-chartered credit unions are not required to meet the credit needs of low- and moderate-income people... as banks are required to do. They have no Community Reinvestment Act (CRA) requirements." [36]

If one is paying close attention, one can see immediately that the wording specifically *doesn't claim that credit unions don't meet the needs of low- and moderate-income people.* It says only that credit unions aren't *required* to do so. The simple reason credit unions aren't required *by law* to meet these needs is because credit unions have historically *always done so*, and do not have the long and well-documented history of exploiting or ignoring underprivileged and underserved groups that *banks* do!

This argument is a little like claiming that it is *unfair* that *law-abiding citizens* aren't required to adhere to the same restrictions that *convicted felons* are. The simple truth is credit unions were *invented* as a cooperative response to the often despicable practices of bankers. [37]

While it may be *technically true* that credit unions are, at times, *not subject to* the same rules that banks are, it is nevertheless *also* true that credit unions *exist* to correct many of the discriminatory injustices that have been perpetuated throughout history by *banks.*

A good example of how the spirit and goals of the CRA are clearly being met by credit unions that are not legally bound to do so is the growth of CDCUs, or Community Development Credit Unions, which serve low-income urban, rural, and reservation-based communities. They range from the smallest of all depositories, with less than $1 million in assets, to credit unions with more than $1 billion in assets, which nevertheless serve predominantly low-income communities.

Most CDCUs and the organizations that support them welcome the ABA's conciliatory position that CDCUs *could* be exempted from any implementation of the CRA for the credit union movement. However, they oppose any proposal to make the CRA applicable to credit unions on the grounds that the massive compliance costs involved could bankrupt credit unions which are already losing money as they attempt to serve a traditionally unprofitable demographic. [38]

Another example of credit unions serving the underserved is their participation in the Community Development Financial Institutions Fund (CDFI Fund) which was created by Congress in 1994 and is administered by the U.S. Treasury Department. Its mission is to expand the capacity of financial institutions to provide credit, capital, and financial services to underserved populations and communities in the United States.

Credit unions, often with the assistance of the National Credit Union Administration (NCUA), may apply for up to $100,000 in Technical Assistance grants to build internal capacity or to achieve CDFI certification. Once certified, CDFI credit unions may apply for up to $2 million in financial assistance for capitalization to support their overall business plan goals of serving underserved communities. One requirement for CDFI certification is that the credit union must serve a low-income demographic. The National Federation of Community Development Credit Unions reported in 2010 that applications for the program have increased by 25% over the previous year. [39]

Still another example is the Community Development Revolving Loan Fund (CDRLF), which is administered by the NCUA. It was established by Congress to support credit unions that serve low-income members and communities by making loans and Technical Assistance Grants (TAGs) available to eligible credit unions. An eligible credit union is one that is federally-chartered and officially designated as a "low-income" credit union (LICU) or a state-chartered credit union with an equivalent low-income designation. [40]

The NCUA also administers the Financial Education Grant Initiative (FEGI), which provides funds to eligible credit unions for collaborative efforts with other community organizations and financial institutions to improve the financial literacy levels of credit union members and community members.

Some specific examples of how the FEGI helps underserved communities include helping credit unions to partner with local immigrant service organizations to provide financial education to non-English speaking community members, working with city and state housing agencies to provide first-time homebuyer counseling and foreclosure prevention counseling, and the funding of basic financial literacy programs in schools and elsewhere in the community. [41]

Some credit unions are taking their community reinvestment efforts directly to the people of their communities or fields of membership. A great example of this is the Pentagon Federal Credit Union Foundation *(The PenFed Foundation),* a nationally-recognized, nonprofit organization whose mission is to meet the unmet needs of military personnel and their families by supporting wounded personnel, and by providing financial management assistance and home ownership assistance.

The foundation is the primary sponsor of the $12.5 million

Defenders Lodge, a facility that, last year alone, provided temporary housing to nearly 11,000 military patients and their families while they waited for medical treatment. Pentagon Federal Credit Union donates all labor expenses for the foundation.

The foundation is dedicated to assisting the men and women of the Department of Defense and Homeland Security and their immediate families, to include uniformed and non-uniformed personnel, many of whom face tremendous financial stress related to their low pay, extended deployments and combat injuries. The PenFed Foundation's also gives no-interest emergency cash loans and free professional counseling to help with the family's money problems.

Despite these and many other initiatives on the part of credit unions to serve the underserved and those of modest means, bankers continue to imply that not only aren't credit unions doing *enough*, but that this failure is because they aren't subject to the CRA.

Many bankers cite a recent Tax Foundation study [42], which concluded that "the credit union tax subsidy has largely failed to deliver financial services to low-income people." Again, this is a very *carefully worded* criticism. Note that the statement tiptoes around the issue of whether *credit unions* are delivering financial services to low-income people. It states specifically that the *"tax subsidy"* hasn't delivered those services, which is an entirely different question altogether. The truth is, it isn't the tax exemption that delivers on this promise, but the very nature and philosophy of the credit union movement itself.

It can fairly be said that the CRA, too, has largely failed to deliver in this regard. A 2006 University of Chicago study looked at "millions of mortgage applications from 1993 to 2003, [and they were] able to distinguish the causal effects of CRA from other (observable and unobservable) variables correlated with residential lending." The study found *"vanishingly small effects* of CRA on the outcomes." In other words, the CRA *made no significant difference* in the low-income neighborhoods studied. [43]

Interestingly enough, a recent study of 600 lending institutions by the Federal Reserve Bank of Kansas found that *98% of their CRA lending was profitable.* [44] Thus, it is entirely conceivable that if the ABA is ever successful in expanding the Community Reinvestment Act in such a way that it applies to credit unions, then they will then have to shift their focus to complaining about how *profitable* the CRA is for them!

"Exceeding Their Mission"

Myth: Credit Unions Are Engaging in Activities that Are Not Part of Their Mission

The nebulous charge that credit unions are exceeding their charter and mission by engaging in activities that belong solely in the domain of banks is typically banker-speak *for "engaging in small business lending."* This spurious charge is often used as a justification for revoking the federal tax exemption for credit unions on the basis that they are no longer acting like credit unions, an argument that was thoroughly discredited in the previous section.

Fact: One in ten Americans is a small businessperson, and small businesses employ 55% of the American workforce. [45]

There can be no discussion of serving the underserved portions of our communities without addressing the need for small business lending. The *very first credit unions*, created in the late 1800s and at the turn of the twentieth century, were organized for the express purpose of meeting small business lending needs, particularly to meet the needs of farmers and other seasonal businesses.

What the bankers have attempted to do, in this particular argument, is *rewrite history.* From the very beginning, the "mission" of credit unions has been to support small businesses.

What is *truly* surprising is the ABA's stance that credit unions are not supporting the needs of underserved communities while simultaneously opposing a proposal that would enhance their ability to do so. An amendment sponsored by Sen. Mark Udall (D-Colo.) which would have raised the business lending cap for credit unions from 12.25% to 27.5% of total assets failed to make it into the Small Business Lending Act of 2010, which was signed into law by President Obama on September 23, 2010. The amendment was scuttled by the banking lobby, which threatened to withhold support for the bill if Udall's amendment was a part of it.

When examining this issue, it is useful to explore the reasons why credit unions have recently increased their member business lending (MBL). According to data published in the American Banker magazine, an examination of the 25 *banks* with the largest business loan portfolios shows that only *two* have reported an increase in business loan portfolio balances over the past year (as of July 2010). In fact, nineteen of the 25 banks reported a double-digit *decline* in their small business lending portfolios.[46]

Banks, in general, are *scaling back* business lending programs or tightening credit criteria, which would put credit unions in the perfect position to meet increasing loan demand, if they were allowed to do so. Business loans for credit unions has increased to 5.21% of their total loan portfolio as of March 31, 2010. [47]

It is ironic that the bankers are claiming that the tax exemption for credit unions should be revoked because credit unions *aren't meeting the needs of the underserved*, even as the bankers themselves are making *far fewer of those kinds of loans* and actively lobbying to prevent *credit unions* from meeting those needs.

The hypocrisy of arguing that credit unions and banks should "play by the same rules" and compete on a "level playing field" becomes even more apparent when it comes to the current Member Business Lending (MBL) cap of 12.25% for credit unions, a cap to which *banks are not subject.*

Predictably, there have been *no* calls from the ABA to make banks subject to the same cap as credit unions, *or* to eliminate the cap for credit unions.

The Bottom Line

Credit unions *must* take immediate steps to counter this *brilliant* public relations campaign by the ABA

Anyone who appreciates the power of marketing and public relations has to appreciate the sheer magnitude, persistence, and genius of this campaign by the ABA, its members, and surrogates. For over 76 years, they have succeeded brilliantly in redefining the verbiage, muddling the core issues, and rewriting history to their advantage. Those in the credit union movement have often become unwitting accomplices in the ABA's campaign by their silence, or at the very least, their acceptance of the ABA's paradigm.

It is increasingly imperative that credit union professionals and volunteers educate themselves and the public about the secret war being waged against credit unions by the ABA and its surrogates, as well as the sophisticated tactics being employed.

It is no longer enough to rely upon the argument that credit unions should remain tax exempt simply because they are not-for-profit financial cooperatives that are controlled by democratically elected boards.

If bankers are allowed to continue, unchallenged, in their efforts to redefine the parameters of the argument and promote their world-view to policy-makers and the public, the eventual outcome will be catastrophic for the credit union movement.

While it is true that the outcomes of recent legislative initiatives have generally supported the credit union view, it is *entirely possible* that the credit union movement has become so focused on the *battle*, they could end up losing the *war*.

A Counter Strategy

It will eventually become necessary to implement a three-tiered strategy to counter the bankers' efforts:

1. **Train** lobbyists, credit union managers, board members, and staffers about the true nature of the campaign being employed against them, the tactics used, and how to respond effectively.

2. **Inform and educate** policy-makers, members of the media, credit union members, and members of the general public through a vigorous campaign that exposes the hypocrisy of the ABA's positions, and *pulls no punches*.

3. **Practice advocacy**. This goes well beyond merely informing and educating. It is the well-known difference between *telling*, and *selling*. Credit union professionals *must* work to hone their persuasive skills and develop greater opportunities for advocacy in their communities and on the national stage.

If the credit union movement is to survive into the 21st century, the "armadillo strategy" of the past will have to be abandoned, and a more aggressive approach emphasizing education, engagement and advocacy adopted. In their desire to "just get along" with our banker-brethren and other influential members of their communities, credit union professionals have often resorted to leaving the "heavy-lifting" to the lobbyists, and hoping, like frightened armadillos, that the issues will simply *go away*.

Unfortunately, hope is *not* a viable strategy, and seriousness of the threat is growing, rather than waning.

Credit union professionals must remain focused on training, informing, educating and advocating *aggressively* to ensure that America's credit unions do *not* follow in the fading footsteps of the nation's Savings & Loans and Thrifts, two financial institutions that have been rendered largely irrelevant by the relentless efforts of the banking lobby. The bankers' tactics have been ingeniously subtle, yet pervasive, and have inflicted significant damage to the credit union movement.

The battlefield is highly complex, and the truth is often difficult to find and organize effectively. It is even more difficult to convey the facts and values of the credit union movement persuasively to policy-makers and the public. It is an on-going mission that must be accomplished, however.

Marcus Aurelius, the second-century Roman Emperor, once said, "The secret of all victory lies in the organization of the non-obvious."

Appendix A: Brief Legislative Timeline

November 24, 1908: St. Mary's Cooperative Credit Association, America's first credit union is founded in Manchester, NH by French-speaking immigrants from Canada.

June 26, 1934: The Federal Credit Union Act established the federal credit union system and created the Bureau of Federal Credit Unions, predecessor to the National Credit Union Administration (NCUA). Its purpose was to make credit available and promote thrift with a national system of nonprofit, cooperative credit unions.

August 10, 1934: The Credit Union National Association (CUNA) was formed as a confederation of state leagues at a meeting in Estes Park, CO. It replaced the Credit Union National Extension Bureau (CUNEB).

1966: The Interest Rate Adjustment Act of 1966, an amendment to Regulation Q, allows thrifts to pay interest rates 50 basis points higher than those of banks.

May 29, 1968: Consumer Credit Protection Act signed into law.

March 10, 1970: President Richard M. Nixon signed Public Law 91, creating the National Credit Union Administration. Previously, credit unions were governed by the Bureau of Federal Credit Unions, which was housed at the Farm Credit Administration.

October 26, 1970: Bank Secrecy Act signed into law.

March 31, 1980: The Depository Institutions Deregulation and Monetary Control Act (DIDMCA) allowed thrifts to make consumer loans up to 20 percent of their assets, issue credit cards, accept negotiable order of withdrawal (NOW) accounts from individuals and nonprofit organizations, and invest up to 20 percent of their assets in commercial real estate loans. This massive deregulation effort was designed, in part, to reverse decades of damage done to the thrift industry by the repeal of their tax exemption in 1951, a collapse in real estate values, and high interest rates.

August 13, 1981: Economic Recovery Tax Act (ERTA). This law is generally viewed as a misguided effort to *help* struggling S&Ls to sell their mortgage loans and use the cash to improve their balance sheets. The losses created by these sales were to be amortized over the life of the loan, and any losses could be offset against their taxes. This made the S&Ls very eager to sell their loans, and experienced Wall Street bankers easily bought most of those loans at 60%-90% of value, bundled them as mortgage-backed government-guaranteed bonds, and sold them back to the S&Ls and others at a substantial profit. There are some who suggest that looting the S&L industry and precipitating the S&L crisis was the hidden agenda of the bankers from the beginning.

October 1, 1982: Garn–St. Germain Depository Institutions Act signed into law, increasing the deregulation of the Savings and Loan industry which led to its eventual collapse.

October 22, 1986: Tax Reform Act of 1986. The law significantly decreased the value of many investments which had been held more for their tax status than for their inherent profitability, hastened the end of the real estate boom of the early '80s, and exacerbated the S&L crisis.

August 9, 1989: Financial Institutions Reform, Recovery and Enforcement Act (*FIRREA*).

August 20, 1996: Congress passes the Small Business Job Protection Act, which allowed insured banks to choose to be taxed as S-corporations effective in 1997. Because S-corporations do not pay federal corporate income taxes, income is transferred directly to stockholders with significant tax savings. For tax purposes, S-corporations are treated as partnerships, with income allocated to stockholders based on the number of shares held. To qualify for Subchapter S status, a bank must be headquartered in the United States and cannot have more than one hundred stockholders, and each stockholder must be an individual, an estate, a qualified plan, or a specific type of tax-exempt organization. Nonresident aliens cannot be stockholders in S-corporation banks, and each bank may have only one class of stock.

February 25, 1998: U.S. Supreme Court decides against the NCUA in *NCUA v. First National Bank & Trust*, which challenged the practice of having multiple common bonds of credit union membership eligibility. This strategic defeat for the NCUA led to the Credit Union Membership Act of 1998.

August 7, 1998: The Credit Union Membership Act signed into law (an amendment to the Credit Union Act of 1934). The amendment allows multiple common bonds for CU fields of membership.

December 4, 2003: Fair and Accurate Credit Transactions (FACT) Act signed into law.

April 20, 2005: Bankruptcy Abuse Prevention and Consumer Protection Act signed into law.

February 8, 2006: Federal Deposit Insurance Reform Act of 2005 enacted, along with the Federal Deposit Insurance Reform Conforming Amendments Act of 2005 on February 15, 2006. It raised the limit on insured deposits to $250,000 per account.

U.S. Financial Crisis of 2007-2010: Poor oversight on the national sub-prime lending market and the subsequent collapse of the so-called "housing bubble," which peaked in 2006, caused a widespread devaluation of housing prices, mortgage-backed securities, and derivatives based on them. This, in turn, threatened the financial viability of many lending institutions, which found themselves with skyrocketing mortgage defaults and increasingly worthless commercial paper.

October 3, 2008: Emergency Economic Stabilization Act of 2008, commonly referred to as the bailout of the U.S. financial system, enacted in response to the subprime mortgage crisis allocating $700 billion to purchase troubled assets, especially mortgage-backed securities, and to make capital injections into banks.

January 28, 2009: The NCUA Corporate Stabilization Program created in response to investment losses incurred at U.S. Central Credit Union, a corporate credit union whose members are limited to retail credit unions.

May 22, 2009: Credit CARD Act signed into law.

May 26, 2009: NCUA $250,000 Share Insurance Protection extended to the year 2013.

July 21, 2010: Dodd–Frank Wall Street Reform and Consumer Protection Act signed into law. It consolidated regulatory agencies, eliminated of the national thrift charter, and created a new oversight council to evaluate systemic risk. Increased regulation of financial markets, improved transparency of derivatives, and created a new consumer protection agency. It implemented the "Volcker Rule," which allows banks to invest up to 3% of their Tier 1 capital in private equity and hedge funds, and to trade for hedging purposes.

September 29, 2010: NCUA regulators guaranteed $80 billion in uninsured deposits at 28 corporate, or wholesale, credit unions. They also injected $1 billion of capital into U.S. Central Federal Credit Union of Lenexa, KS, the largest corporate credit union, after the firm posted an unexpected $1.1 billion loss for 2008.

Appendix B: Recommended Reading

Banking Taxation: Implications of Proposed Revisions Governing S-Corporations on Community Banks, *United States General Accounting Office*, June 2000
http://www.gao.gov/archive/2000/gg00159.pdf

Community Reinvestment Act, FFIEC Website,
http://www.ffiec.gov/cra/

CUNA Issue Summary: Subchapter S Corporation Banks, *Credit Union National Association,* August 25, 2010.
http://www.cuna.org/gov_affairs/legislative/issues/download/sub_s _banks.pdf

On the Uniqueness of Community Banks, Federal Reserve Bank of Atlanta, Scott E. Hein, Timothy W. Koch, and Scott Macdonald, Economic Review 1QTR 2005
http://finance.ba.ttu.edu/hein/Research Papers/On the Uniqueness of Community Banks.pdf

Requiem for Regulation Q: What It Did and Why It Passed Away, *St. Louis Federal Reserve,* R. Alton Gilbert.
http://research.stlouisfed.org/publications/review/86/02/Requiem_ Feb1986.pdf

The Impact of Tax Law Changes on Bank Dividend Policy, Sell-offs, Organizational Form, and Industry Structure, *Federal Reserve Bank of New York Staff Reports,* Hamid Mehran and Michael Suher, (Staff Report #369) April 2009. http://www.newyorkfed.org/research/staff_reports/sr369.pdf

Appendix C: Glossary of Acronyms

ABA. American Bankers Association founded in 1875 and headquartered in Washington D.C.

BFCU. Bureau of Federal Credit Unions, a regulatory predecessor to the NCUA.

CDCU. Community Development Credit Unions; which serve low-income urban, rural, and reservation-based communities.

CDFI. Community Development Financial Institutions Fund (CDFI Fund); administered by the U.S. Treasury Department to assist financial institutions in serving the underserved.

CRA. Community Reinvestment Act. Part of the Housing and Community Development Act of 1977. It addressed historical discrimination on the part of banks in low and moderate-income neighborhoods. The CRA does not require financial institutions to make financially unsound loans. (43)

CDRLF. Community Development Revolving Loan; administered by the NCUA to support credit unions that serve low-income members and communities by making loans and Technical Assistance Grants.

CUNA. Credit Union National Association, a national trade association for state- and federally-chartered credit unions. Provides member CUs with lobbying, professional development, and professional services management. Headquartered in

Washington, D.C., with an operations center in Madison, WI.

CUNEB. Credit Union National Extension Bureau, predecessor organization to CUNA.

DIDMCA. Depository Institutions Deregulation and Monetary Control Act of 1980. (See Appendix A)

EESA. The Emergency Economic Stabilization Act of 2008 (aka "The Financial System Bailout")

FDIC. Federal Deposit Insurance Corporation, a US government corporation created by the Glass-Steagall Act of 1933. It insures deposits, examines and supervises banks for safety and soundness, and manages banks in receivership.

FEGI. Financial Education Grant Initiative; a financial literacy program of the NCUA designed to fund education in low-income or underserved areas.

FFIEC. Federal Financial Institutions Examination Council.

FHFA. Federal Housing Finance Agency.

FHLMC. Freddie Mac, or the Federal Home Loan Mortgage Corporation.

FIRREA. Financial Institutions Reform, Recovery and Enforcement Act of 1989 (FIRREA) (See Appendix A).

FNMA. Fannie Mae, or the Federal National Mortgage Association.

FOM. Field of Membership, or the common bonds upon which eligibility for CU membership may be based.

GSE. Government Sponsored Enterprise.

LICU. Low-Income Credit Union; an NCUA designation for credit unions where a majority of their members fit the low-income demographic.

MBL. Member Business Lending; small business loans made to credit union members.

NCUA. National Credit Union Administration, an independent federal agency that supervises and charters federal credit unions. It also insures deposits in all federal (and most state-chartered) credit unions through the NCUSIF.

NCUF. The credit union movement's primary national charitable fundraising organization for credit union development. An affiliate of the Credit Union National Association (CUNA).

NCUSIF. National Credit Union Share Insurance Fund; managed by the NCUA.

OTS. Office of Thrift Supervision; An office within the Treasury Department that supervises the thrift industry (savings & loans associations).

SMSIA. Standard Maximum Share Insurance Amount.

TAG. Technical Assistance Grant; support for low-income credit unions by the NCUA.

TARP. Troubled Asset Relief Program, a $700 billion program to purchase failing bank assets as part of EESA (aka "The Financial System Bailout").

UBIT. Unrelated Business Income Tax. A tax that is levied on income which comes from an activity engaged in by a tax-exempt organization that is not related to the tax-exempt purpose of that organization.

WOCCU. World Council of Credit Unions, an international trade association for credit unions. Headquartered in Madison, Wisconsin, their members include regional and national credit union associations, co-op associations and business service organizations in 97 countries.

About the Author

Michael McKelly has worked for financial institutions for over ten years, and has been employed by both banks and credit unions as a marketing director, product development specialist, business development officer, and public relations officer. He has many years of experience in community outreach and as a public speaker on the topics of banking, wealth management, the real costs of credit, and credit union advocacy.

Michael is a veteran of 20 years of active duty military service with the United States Army, a former magazine publisher, freelance writer, and author of two previous books in other genres.

His hobbies and interests include travel, languages, koi ponds, skiing, skydiving, and Scrabble.

He currently resides in Wichita Falls, Texas.

End Notes

[1] U.S. Supreme Court, 1998.

[2] The Credit Union Membership Access Act of 1998, HR 1151, was signed into law by the President on August 7, 1998. This Act authorizes multiple-group chartering for Federal credit unions.

[3] American Bankers Association, http://www.aba.com/Industry+Issues/Issues_CU_Menu.htm

[4] The Federal Reserve Board, Community Reinvestment Act, http://www.federalreserve.gov/dcca/cra/

[5] Credit Union National Association, http://www.cuna.org/gov_affairs/legislative/cu_difference.html

[6] Credit Union National Association, http://www.cuna.org/gov_affairs/legislative/cu_difference.html

[7] S-Corporation Status Under the Microscope, America's Community Banker magazine, Author: Michelle Clayton, March 1, 1998

[8] S Corporation Banks on the Rise, http://www.allbusiness.com/north-america/united-states-texas/1037322-1.html

[9] Federal Reserve Bank of Atlanta, On the Uniqueness of Community Banks, Scott E. Hein, Timothy W. Koch, and Scott Macdonald, 2003, http://finance.ba.ttu.edu/hein/Research Papers/On the Uniqueness of Community Banks.pdf

[10] Credit Union National Association, http://www.cuna.org/gov_affairs/legislative/issues/download/sub_s_banks.pdf

[11] On the Uniqueness of Community Banks, Federal Reserve Bank of Atlanta, Scott E. Hein, Timothy W. Koch, and Scott Macdonald, Economic Review 1QTR 2005 http://finance.ba.ttu.edu/hein/Research Papers/On the Uniqueness of Community Banks.pdf

[12] Federal Deposit Insurance Corporation, http://www.FDIC.gov

[13] Kansas City Federal Reserve Bank, http://www.kansascityfed.org/publicat/fip/prs03-2.pdf

[14] Credit Union National Association, http://www.cuna.org/download/ra_cu_size_analysis.pdf

[15] Federal Deposit Insurance Corporation, http://www.FDIC.gov

[16] U.S. Senate Report No. 781, 1951-2 C.B. 476

[17] Reference for Business, http://www.referenceforbusiness.com/encyclopedia/Res-Sec/Savings-and-Loan-Associations.html

[18] Lessons From the Savings and Loan Debacle, Catherine England, Cato Institute, http://www.cato.org/pubs/regulation/regv15n3/reg15n3-england.html

[19] Housing Finance in Developed Countries: An International Comparison of Efficiency,   Douglas B. Diamond, Jr. and Michael J. Lea, FannieMae Foundation, http://www.knowledgeplex.org/kp/text_document_summary/scholarly_article/relfiles/jhr_0301_hfdc.html

[20] Credit Union National Association, http://www.cuna.org/initiatives/growth_membership/member/summary.pdf

[21] Massachusetts Bankers Association, "The Credit Union Ruse: Can Credit Unions Legitimately Claim They Shouldn't Pay Taxes?" http://www.creditunionruse.com/

[22] National Credit Union Administration (NCUA), http://www.ncua.gov

[23] Massachusetts Bankers Association, "The Credit Union Ruse: Can Credit Unions Legitimately Claim They Shouldn't Pay Taxes?" http://www.creditunionruse.com/

[24] Tax Foundation, http://www.taxfoundation.org/files/corporate_income_taxes_cost_families-20080818.pdf

[25] New York Stock Exchange, http://www.nyse.com/about/listed/lcddata.html?ticker=MCD

[26] TARP Deadbeat List Keeps Growing, Lauren Tara LaCapra, The Street, 9/17/2010. http://www.thestreet.com/story/10864698/1/tarp-deadbeat-list-keeps-growing.html

[27] Wall Street Journal, "Credit Unions Bailed Out", 9/25/2010, http://online.wsj.com/article/SB1000142405274870349960457551225406368 2236.html

[28] National Credit Union Administration (NCUA), "Understanding the Corporate Crisis," http://www.ncua.gov/Resources/CorporateCU/CSR/Presentations.aspx

[29] National Credit Union Administration (NCUA), "Understanding the Corporate Crisis," http://www.ncua.gov/Resources/CorporateCU/CSR/Presentations.aspx

[30] Massachusetts Bankers Association, "The Credit Union Ruse: Can Credit Unions Legitimately Claim They Shouldn't Pay Taxes?" http://www.creditunionruse.com/

[31] Cornell University Law School, U.S. Code, http://www.law.cornell.edu/uscode/12/usc_sup_01_12.html

[32] 12 U.S.C. § 1757(6), CUNA Model Credit Union Act § 0.70, (2007)

[33] 12 U.S.C. § 1757, CUNA Model Credit Union Act § 3.10, (2007)

[34] 12 U.S.C. § 1760, CUNA Model Credit Union Act § 4.90 (2007)

[35] 12 U.S.C. §§ 1760-1761b, CUNA Model Credit Union Act §§ 5.15-5.20 (2007)

[36] The National Federation of Community Development Credit Unions, http://www.cdcu.coop/i4a/pages/index.cfm?pageid=992

[37] World Council of Credit Unions, What is a Credit Union? http://www.woccu.org/about/creditunion/

[38] National Credit Union Administration (NCUA), The National Federation of Community Development Credit Unions, http://www.cuna.org/newsnow/10/system071210-3.html

[39] National Credit Union Administration (NCUA), http://www.ncua.gov/resources/credituniondevelopment/finance.aspx

[40] National Credit Union Administration (NCUA), http://www.ncua.gov/resources/credituniondevelopment/Files/Programs/ Grants/2010/6060.pdf

[41] Credit Union Times, http://www.cutimes.com/Issues/2010/September- 22-2010/Pages/Senate-Passes-Lending-Bill-but-Eschews-MBL- Hike.aspx

[42] The Community Reinvestment Act: A Regression Discontinuity Analysis, by Christopher R. Berry and Sarah L. Lee, http://harrisschool.uchicago.edu/about/publications/working- papers/pdf/wp_07_04.pdf

[43] Credit Union National Association, http://www.cuna.org/download/ra_cu_size_analysis.pdf

[44] Larry Meeker and Forest Myers, Community Reinvestment Act Lending: Is it Profitable? Financial Industry Perspectives , Federal Reserve Bank of Kansas City, 1996, pp. 13-45

[45] Tax Foundation, http://www.taxfoundation.org/

[46] Credit Unions.com, http://www.creditunions.com/article.aspx?articleid=3798

[47] National Federation of Independent Business, http://www.411sbfacts.com/speeches.html#q1

www.ingramcontent.com/pod-product-compliance
Lightning Source LLC
Chambersburg PA
CBHW070334290526
45791CB00003B/1319